My Beastly book of Hilarious Heroes

Owlkids Books Inc.
10 Lower Spadina Avenue, Suite 400, Toronto, Ontario M5V 2Z2
www.owlkids.com

North American edition © 2011 Owlkids Books Inc.

Published in France under the title *Mon cahier de super-héros* © 2011, Éditions Milan
300 rue Léon-Joulin, 31101 Toulouse Cedex 9, France
www.editionsmilan.com

Library and Archives Canada Cataloguing in Publication

Boudgourd, Vincent
        My beastly book of hilarious heroes : 150 ways to doodle, scribble, color
and draw / Vincent Boudgourd.

ISBN 978-1-926973-01-2

        1. Drawing books--Juvenile literature. I. Title.

NC655.B676 2011   j741.2   C2011-900369-4

Library of Congress Control Number: 2010943325

Canada Council   Conseil des Arts   ONTARIO ARTS COUNCIL
for the Arts   du Canada   CONSEIL DES ARTS DE L'ONTARIO

We acknowledge the financial support of the Canada Council for the Arts, the Ontario
Arts Council, the Government of Canada through the Canada Book Fund (CBF), and
the Government of Ontario through the Ontario Media Development Corporation's
Book Initiative for our publishing activities.

Manufactured by C & C Offset Printing Co.
Manufactured in Shenzhen, China in March 2011
Job #2101275R5

A   B   C   D   E   F

OWl kids   Publisher of Chirp, chickaDEE and OWL
           www.owlkids.com

Meet the Hilarious Heroes!
They're the enemies of evil!

The protectors of the people! The savers of the world!

Too bad they're also a bunch of scaredy cats,
show-offs and clumsy sleepyheads.

In other words, they really need your help.

It's time to grab your own gadgets of justice,
and whip these heroes into shape!

So read each instruction, and let your imagination go.
After all, **you're a superhero, too!**

Draw a **pile of cars** on the
little finger of Super-strong Man.

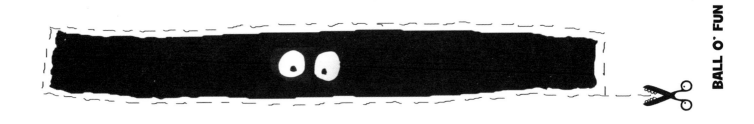

Cut out this page and the black mask for the Bandit Ball.
Scrunch the rest of the page into a ball, glue on the mask,
and throw the Bandit Ball to make him fly!

Superheroes need vacations, too!
Finish the palm tree and color in the sunset.

Draw **umbrellas** for these superheroes.

Draw lots more **rain**, too!

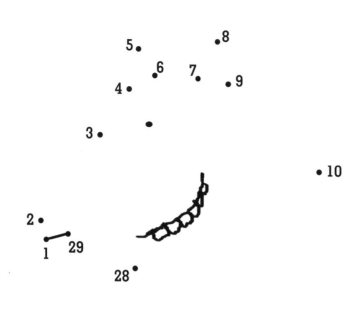

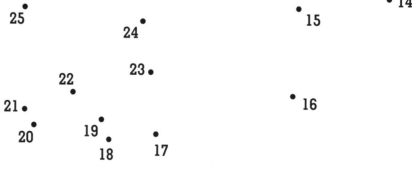

Connect the dots to make
Super-Invisible appear.

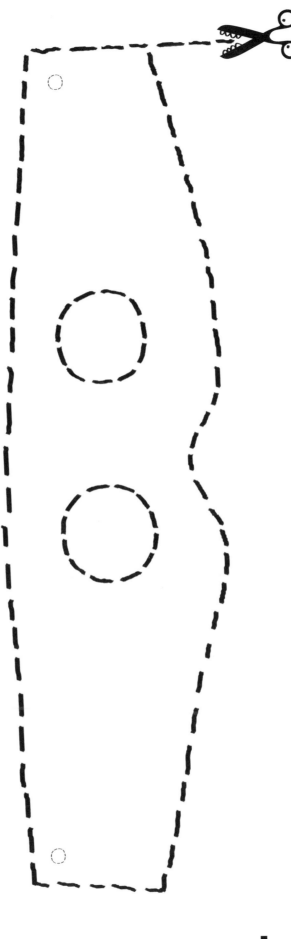

Color and cut out this **mask**, then wear it.

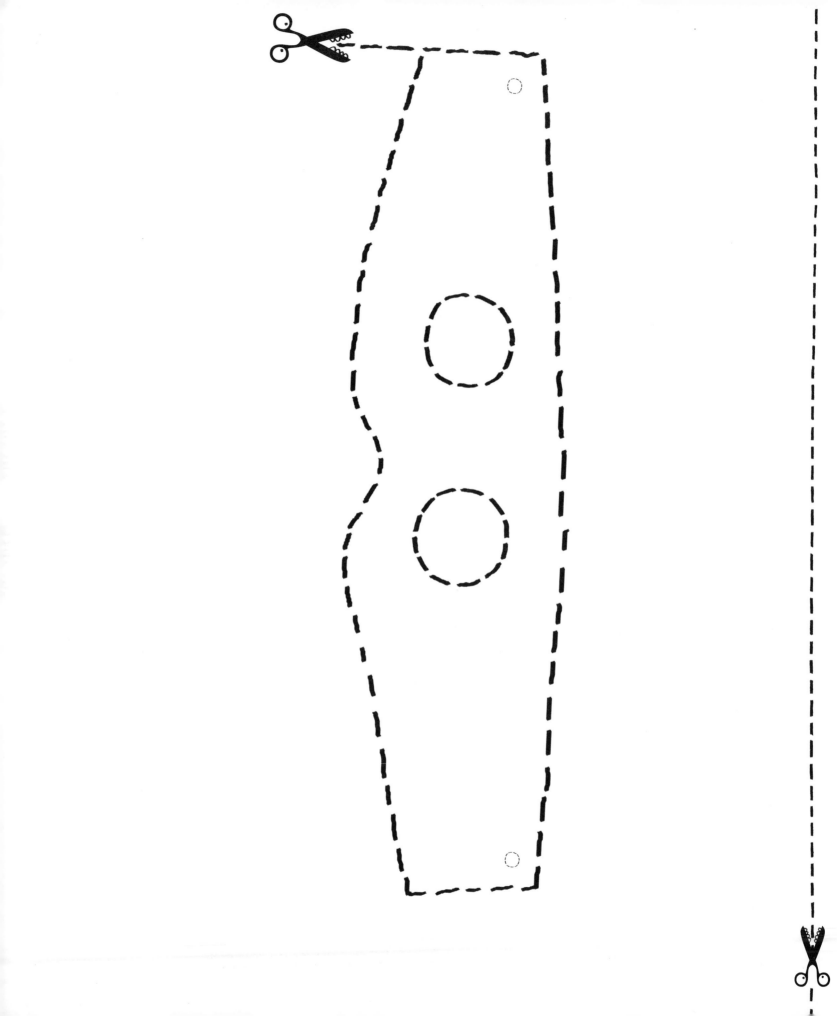

The Lunk is **angry**.
Finish the bars to shut him in the cage.

This superheroine is the queen of **loop-de-loops**.

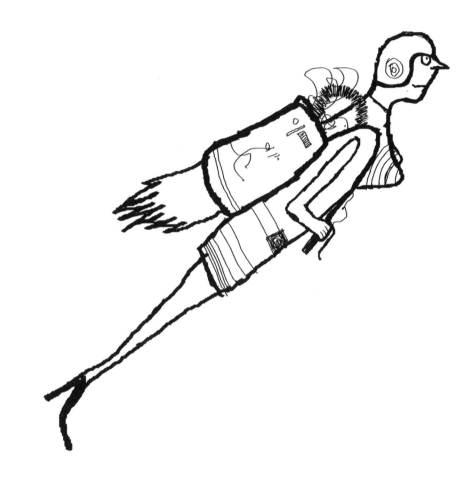

Draw the smoke **trail** she's left behind her.

Are you **right-handed?** Color this in with your left hand.
Are you **left-handed?** Color this in with your right hand.

Draw the rest of **Super-Blob's** gooey body.

Target Man has lost his friend. Help him cross the sky

while avoiding the clouds and meteors.

Draw lots of **flies** in the web of the Web Master.

Cut out, color and send this **postcard** to your favorite superhero. Write a nice note, then make up the address.

Attack Mega-Glutton with **tons of candy.**

The **Crazy Cane** has an amazing laser cane.

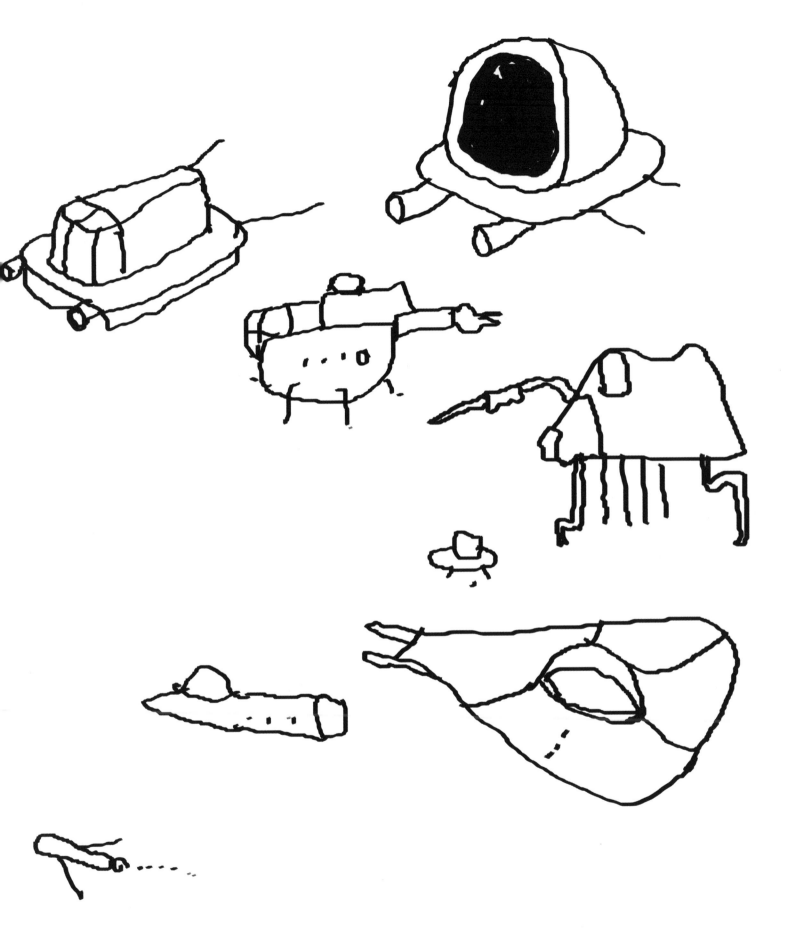

Draw beams from it to destroy the enemy ships.

Super-Pilot is preparing for takeoff!

But where is his rocket? Draw it for him.

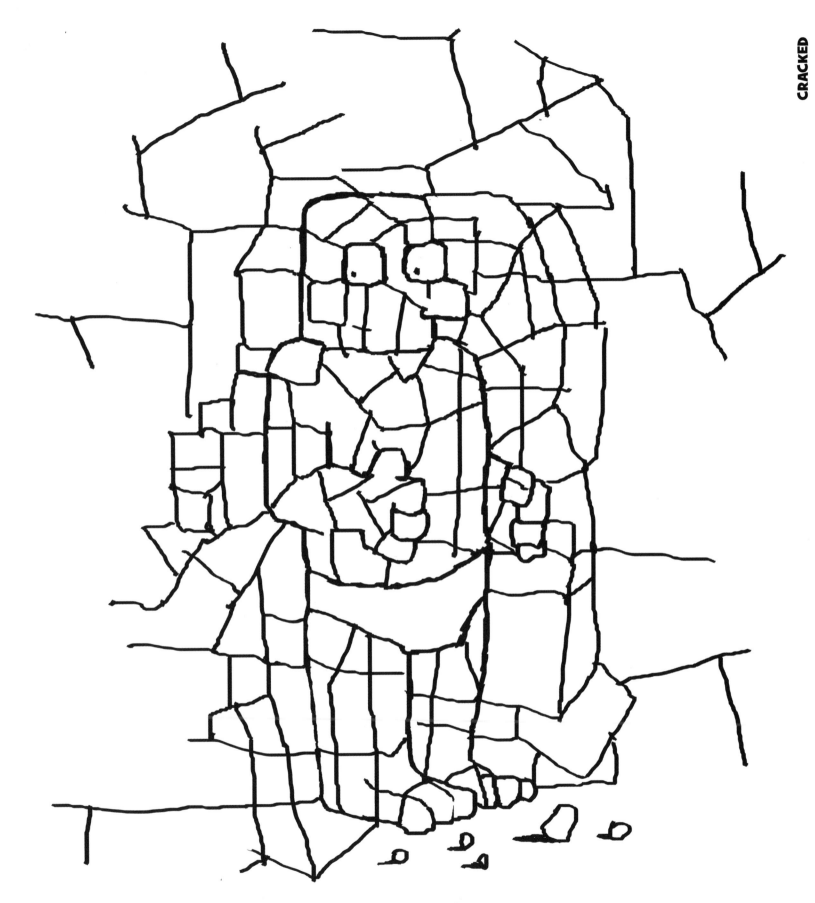

Find the **Human Stone** in the picture and color him bright pink.

Draw these silly superheroes' silly **jetpacks**

so they can take off!

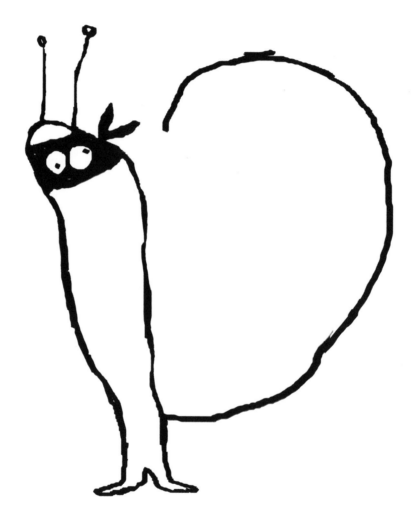

Draw a **ninja snail** tossing a pizza.

What happens in a monster's cave?
Cut out the keyhole and take a peek.

Help the tiny superhero fight the giant monster
with a **cloud of bubbles.**

Which one is the **hero**?

Circle him.

Change this ordinary **family** into a family of heroes!

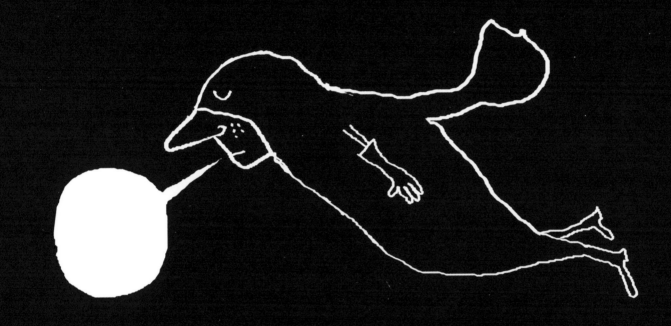

Help Super-Invisible disappear by coloring the page **black**.

Draw the waves that the Golden Surfer is riding on.

Cut out this sign, color it in and attach it to your bedroom door.

Create a four-color hairdo for Ultra-Bizzaro.

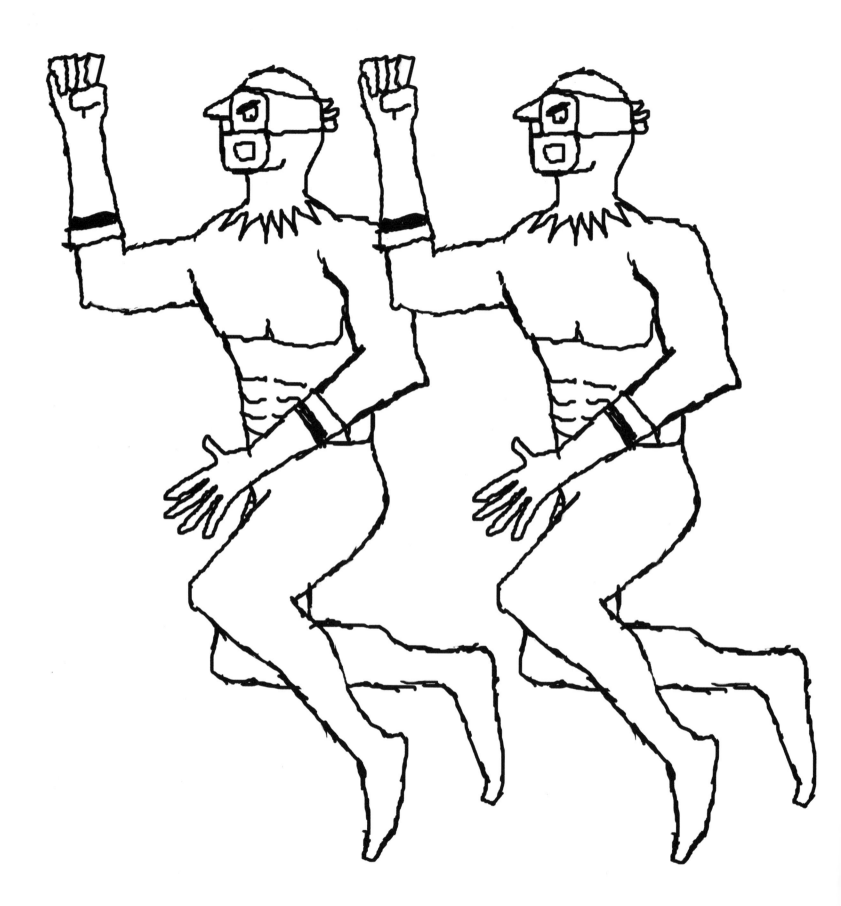

Color in: THE PURPLE POWER   THE GREAT GREENIE

THE OMEGA ORANGE   and THE RED ROCKET

Find the path that will lead Beetle-Man to the exit

EXIT

without touching any of the **branches.**

Defy Super-Janitor. Make this **bathroom** a mess.

Draw the huge head of **Super-Zero.**

Tornado Girl was just here. Finish drawing the swirls

and color in the lightning **flashes**.

Draw **claws** on this werewolf so he can fight.

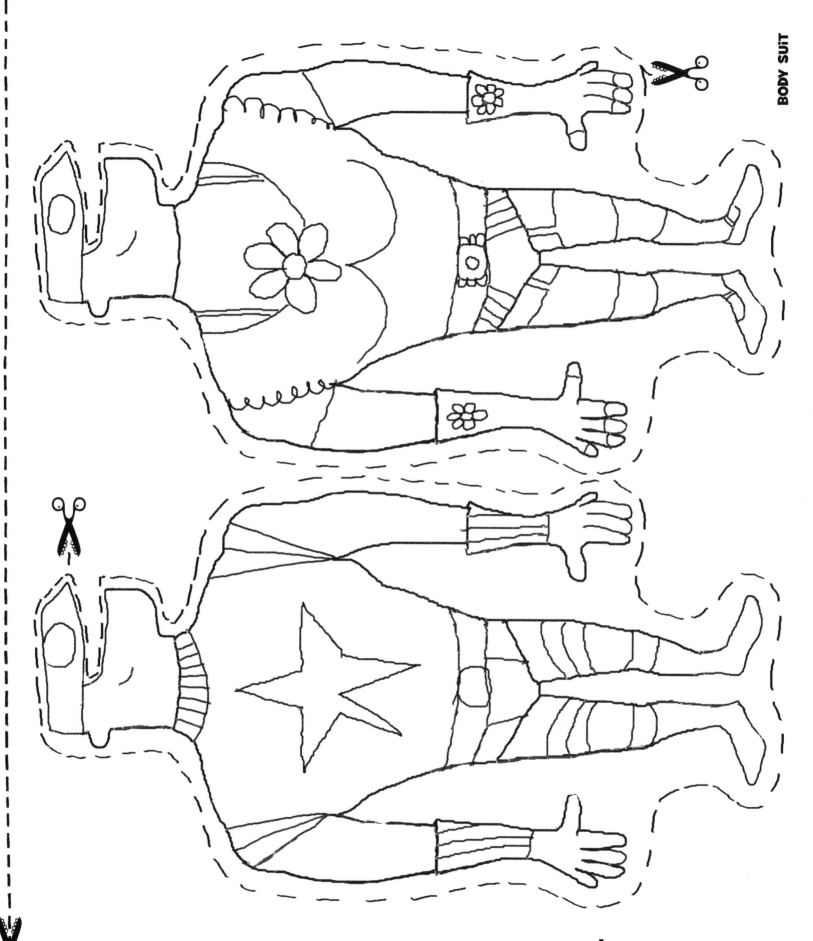

Color and cut out your favorite costume.

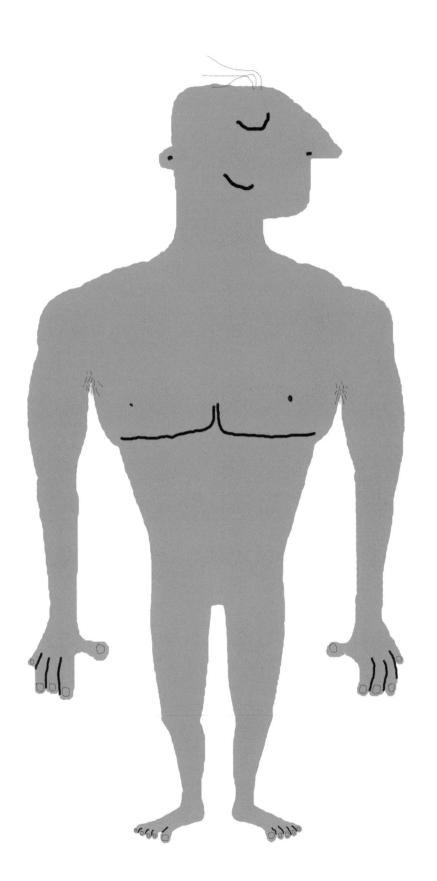

Now you can dress **Super-Strong**. Glue your costume here.

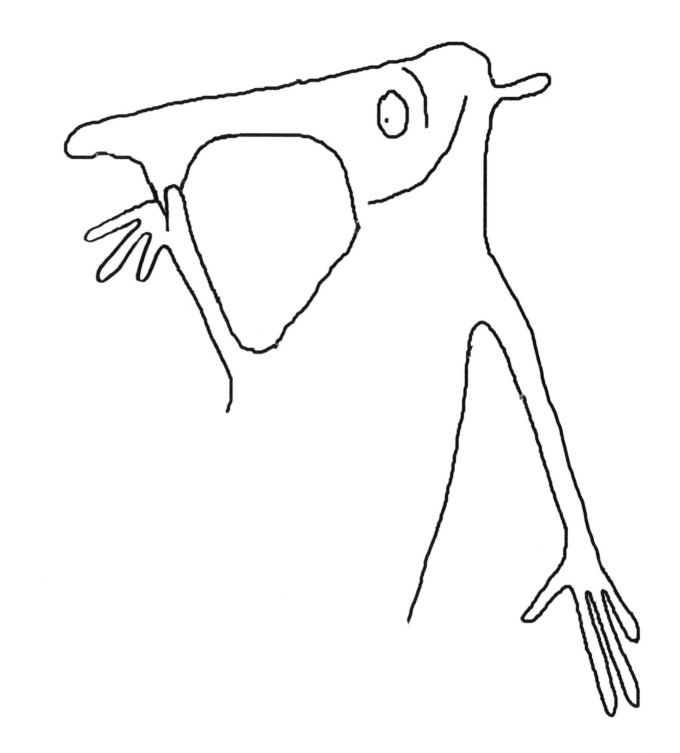

Finish drawing **Elasto-Boy's** body.

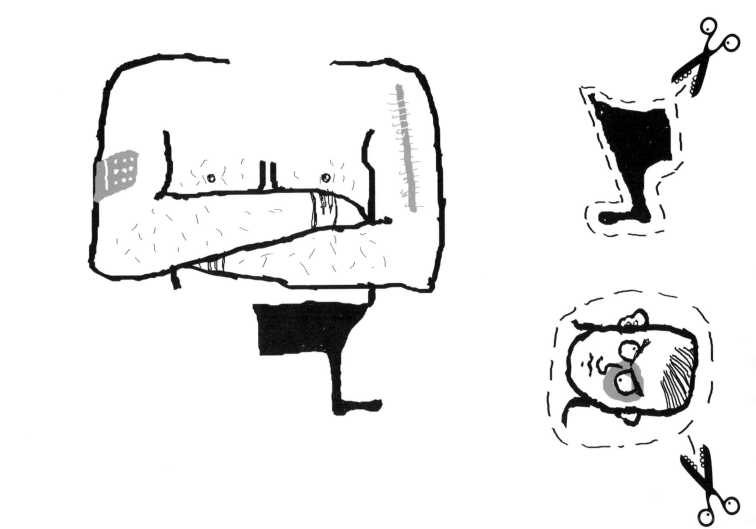

Cut and paste the Bruiser's head and leg in the right place.

Draw **yourself** as the hero of your dreams.

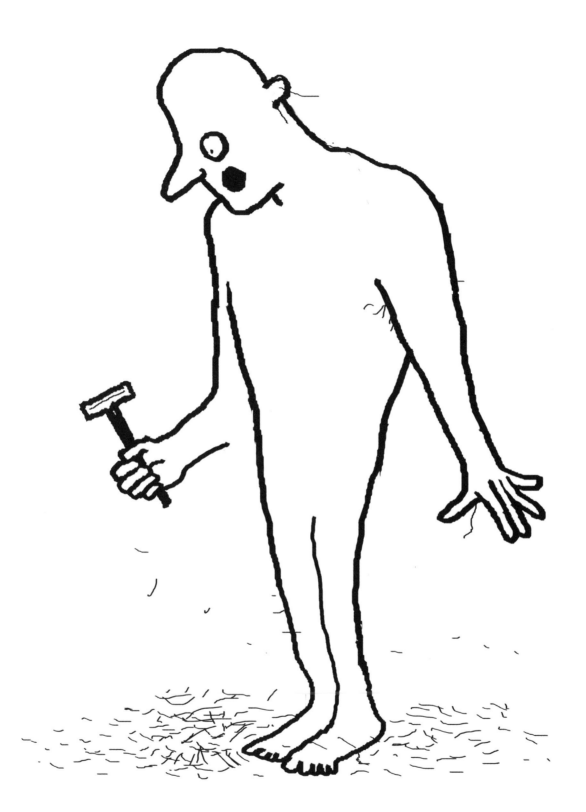

Ape-Man shaved off all his hair...but that took away all his super powers! Draw hair all over his body.

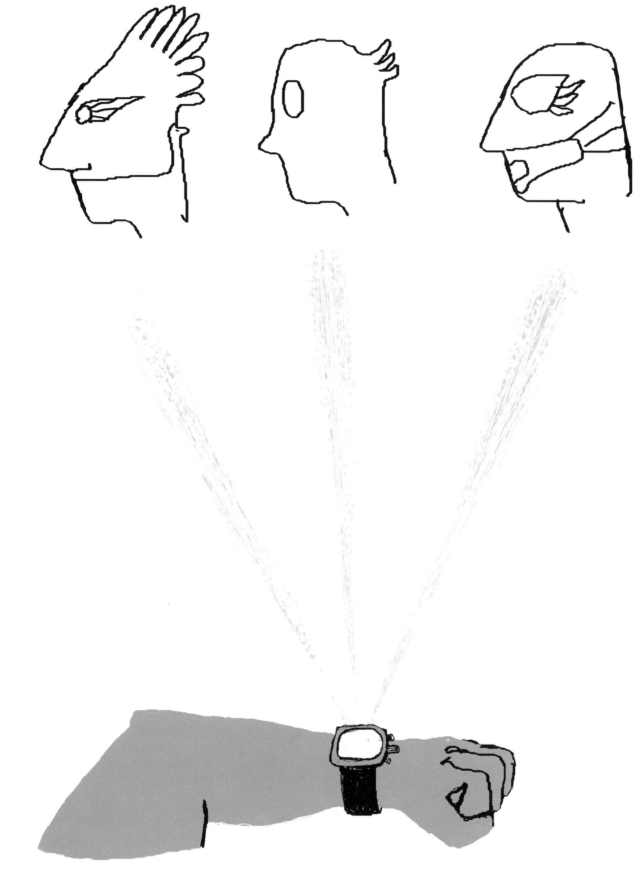

Complete the three **holographic** superheroes and color them in.

Scribble Mr. Focus's eyebeams to explode the **evil** monster.

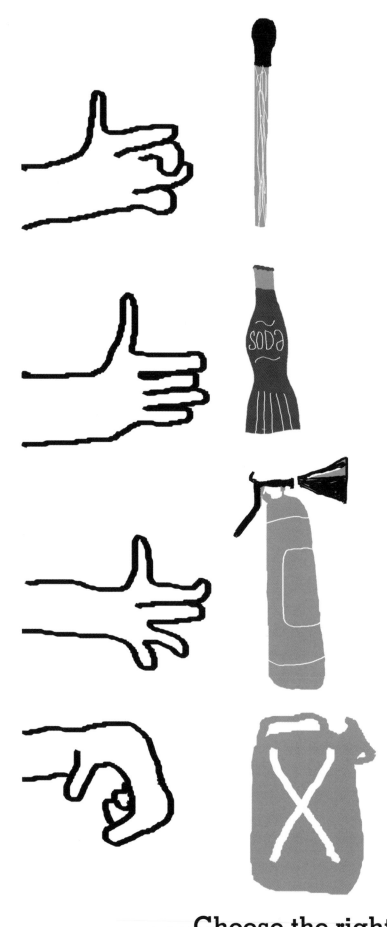

Choose the right weapon to fight

the Ferocious Flame and put it into action.

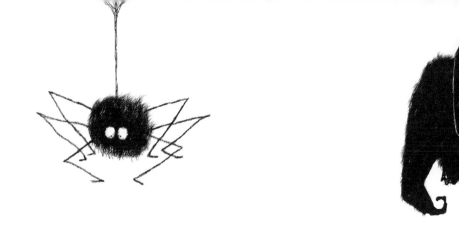

Lots of superheroes copy **animals.** What would

Super-Spider, Super-Gorilla, Super-Zebra and Super-Skunk wear?

Add a head and hands to the angry **villain** trapped in a wall.

It's a day off! Color in the super-things
this superhero puts in his **super-basket**.

Imagine what a villain made of **lasagna** looks like.
What is its name?

¡ JUST ¡RONED THAT!

Crumple the cape of Ironing Man by **crumpling** the page.

Color this **mega-bomb** to look like a giant gumball.

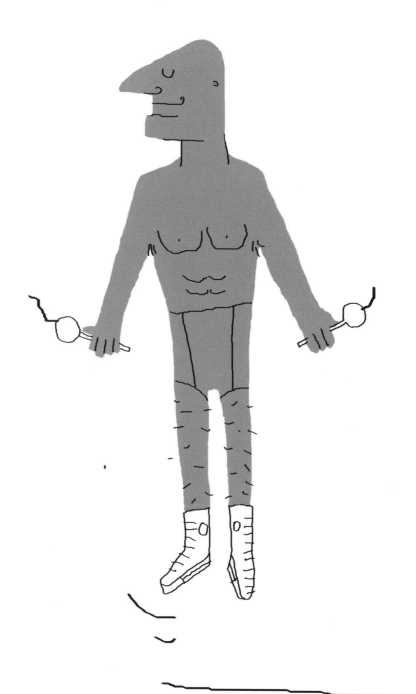

Superheroes need to train, too!

Draw **jump ropes** for them.

Draw 4 more metal arms for PoolPus, the **Octo-Bot.**

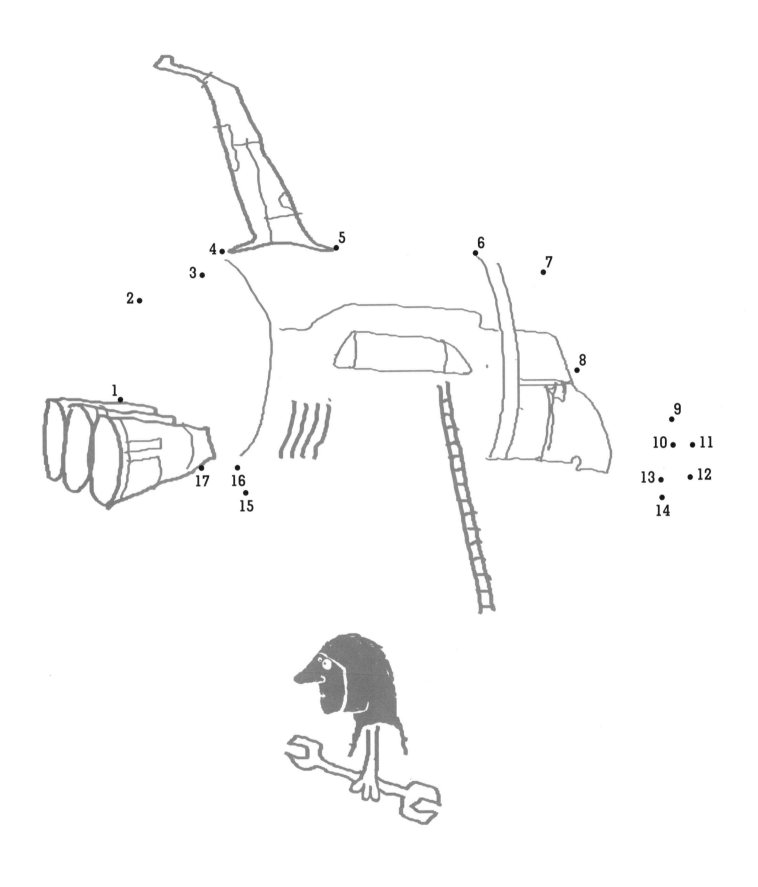

Help Fix-It Man repair his ship by connecting the dots.

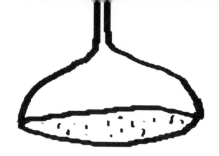

Turn on the **shower** for Mr. Mini-Match.

Color these super-bracelets, cut them out and wear them on your wrists. What **powers** do they give you?

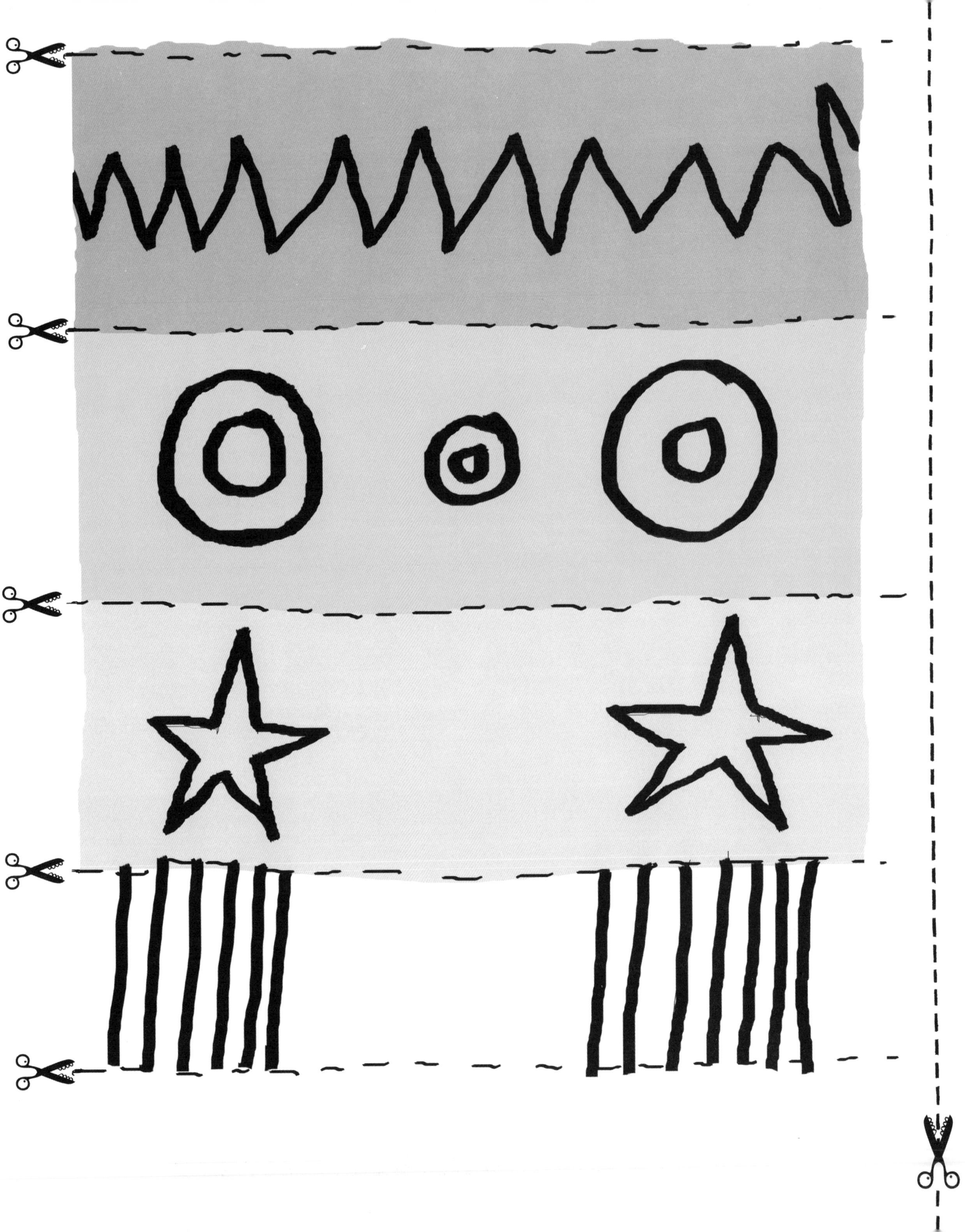

Add some mega-muscles to Mega-Buff.

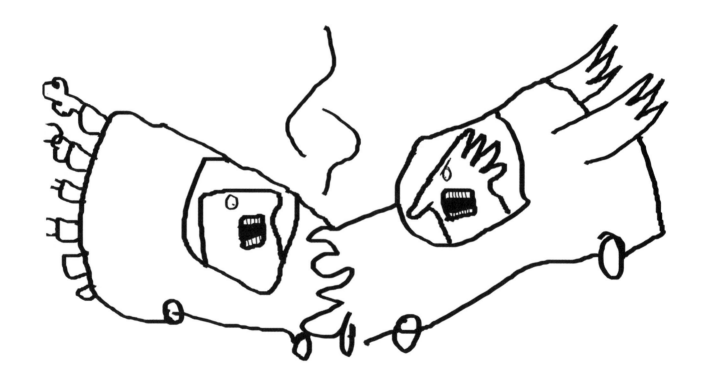

**Super-Speedy and Super-Roadhog have crashed.
Draw the flames, the smoke and the sparks.**

Draw a laser beam coming from Super-Make-Up's **lipstick.**

Circle all of the **differences**

between these two pictures.

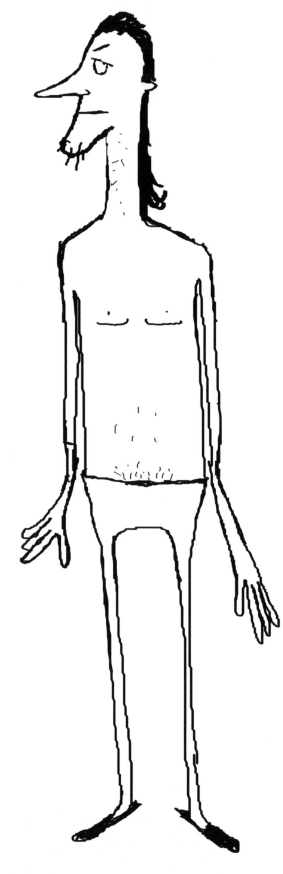

Draw mighty **armor** for Shrimp Man.

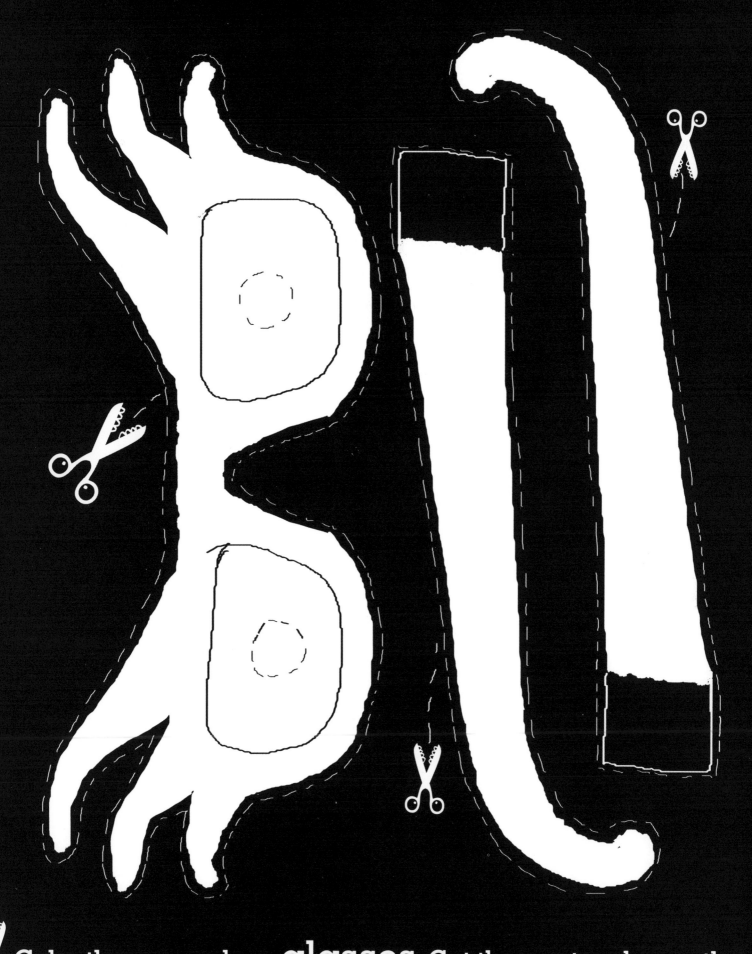

Color these superhero **glasses**. Cut them out and wear them.

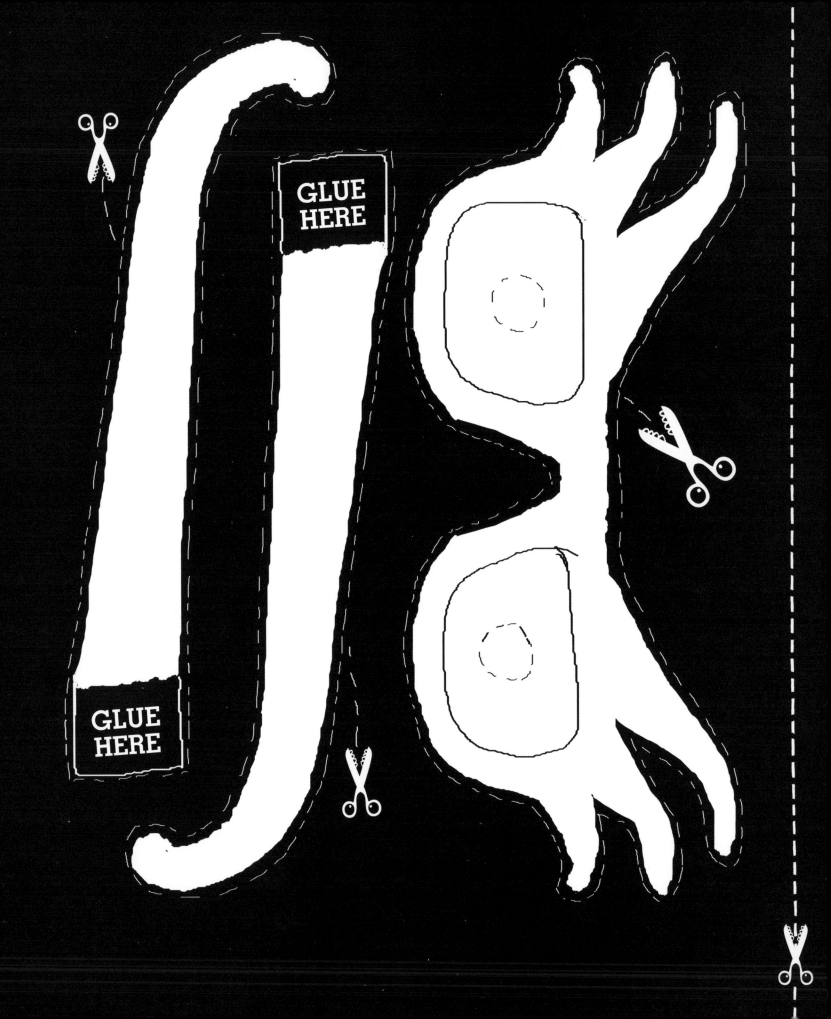

GLUE HERE

GLUE HERE

Draw a superhero as he vacuums up **evil army ants**.

Draw your head here.
You can be even stronger than the superheroes!

Draw your nasty **arch-enemy** here.

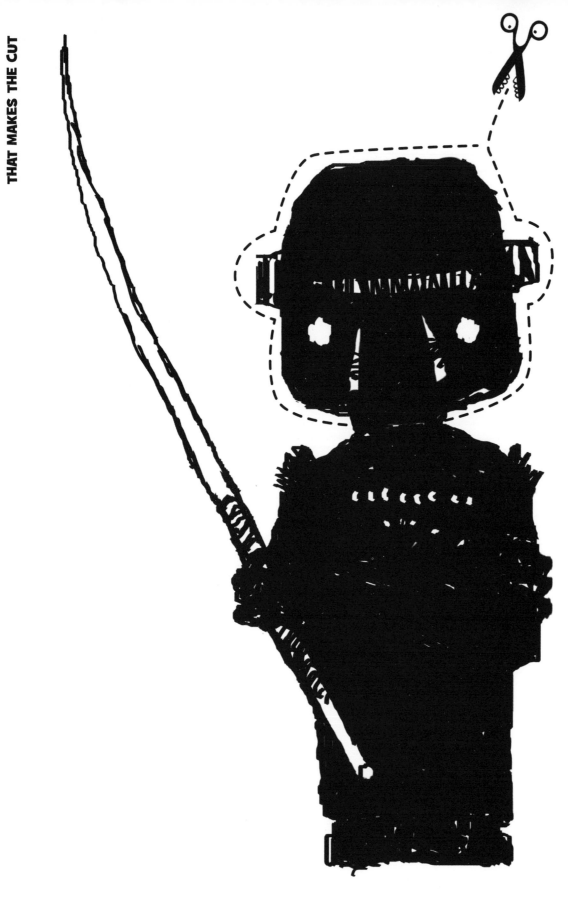

Cut out the mask to see who the **Super-Ninja** is.
Do you recognize that person?

Draw some superheroes from the **Middle Ages** to help this knight.

Play a joke on Brain-Buster.
Color in his **mask** so he can't see.

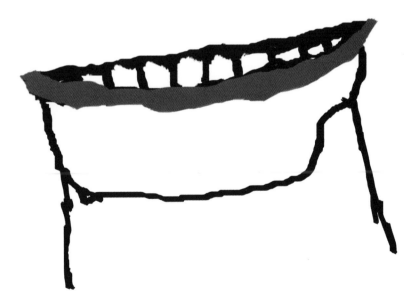

Lunk, the green giant, is very hungry.
Give him a huge **cob of corn** to eat.

Can the bad guy escape

through the **web** of the Web Master? Find out!

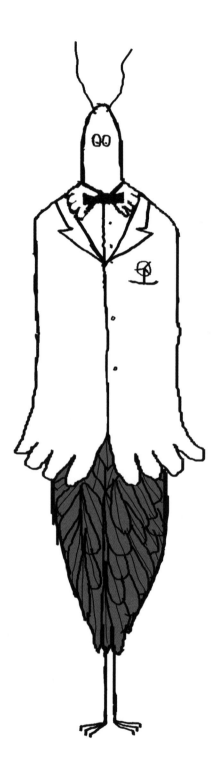

Fly-Man is going out tonight.
Draw him some fancy **butterfly** wings.

Balloon Brain has a rather big head.
Pop it all over with your pen.

Pssssssst! Oops! Well, color in Balloon Brain anyway.

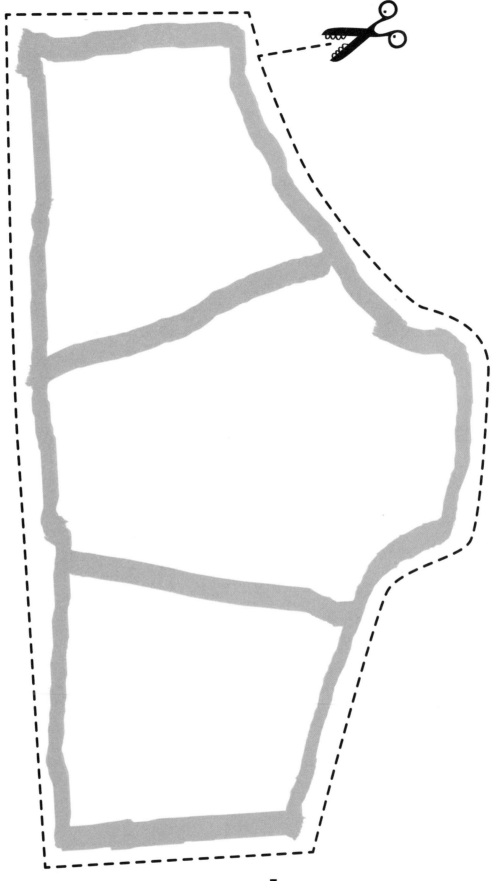

Imagine your superhero underwear. Color them, cut them out, then hide them in your mother's purse.

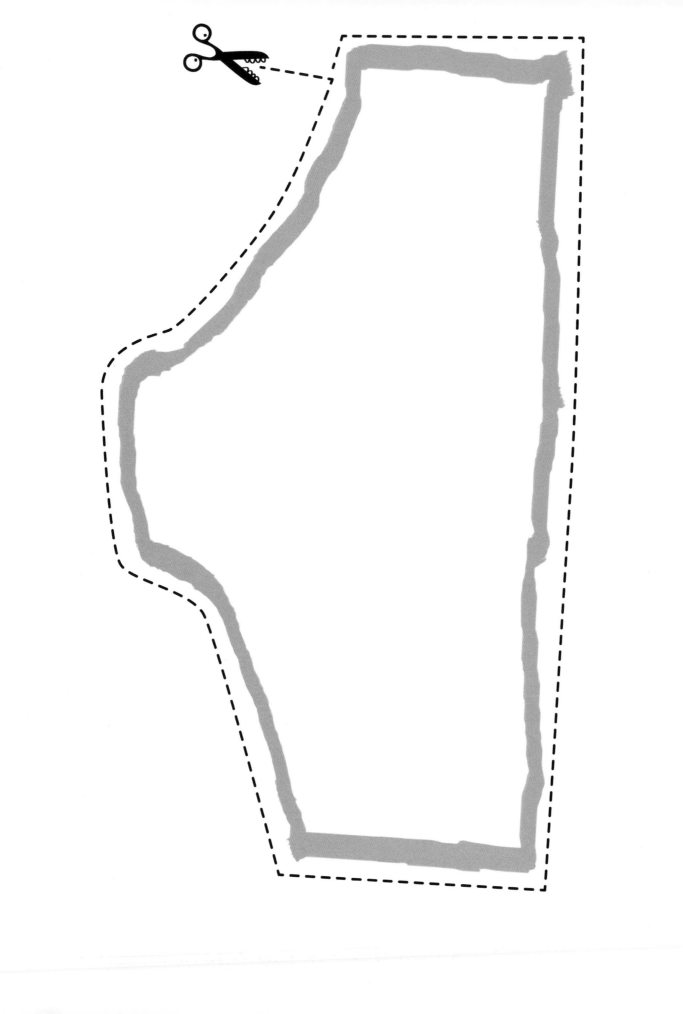

Draw spaghetti sauce coming out of Big-Spaghetti's water gun.

Mr. Q is **angry**. Which of his superhero students

started the fire in the garbage can? Give him a dunce cap.

This **hero** wants to go unnoticed.
Give him some glasses, a beard and a hat.

Put your foot on the page. Trace it with a black marker, **pressing hard**, then turn the page.

Yikes! You've squashed Super-Invisible!

This superhero flew too close to the sun.
Color in his **sunburn**.

3.

.6

4.

.5

oo

1. pmmm .8

.7

2.

**Connect the dots to see what's
got Captain Scaredy-Cat so frightened.**

Draw a SCARY mouse.

Draw what you think the evil villain
the **Big Cheese** looks like.

Now draw his **partner**, Milk Shake.

The **washroom** is occupied. Color this page while you wait.

washroom

**Hey! You've been waiting for 3 hours!
Knock on the door and open it.**

Finally! Draw some graffiti on the bathroom door.

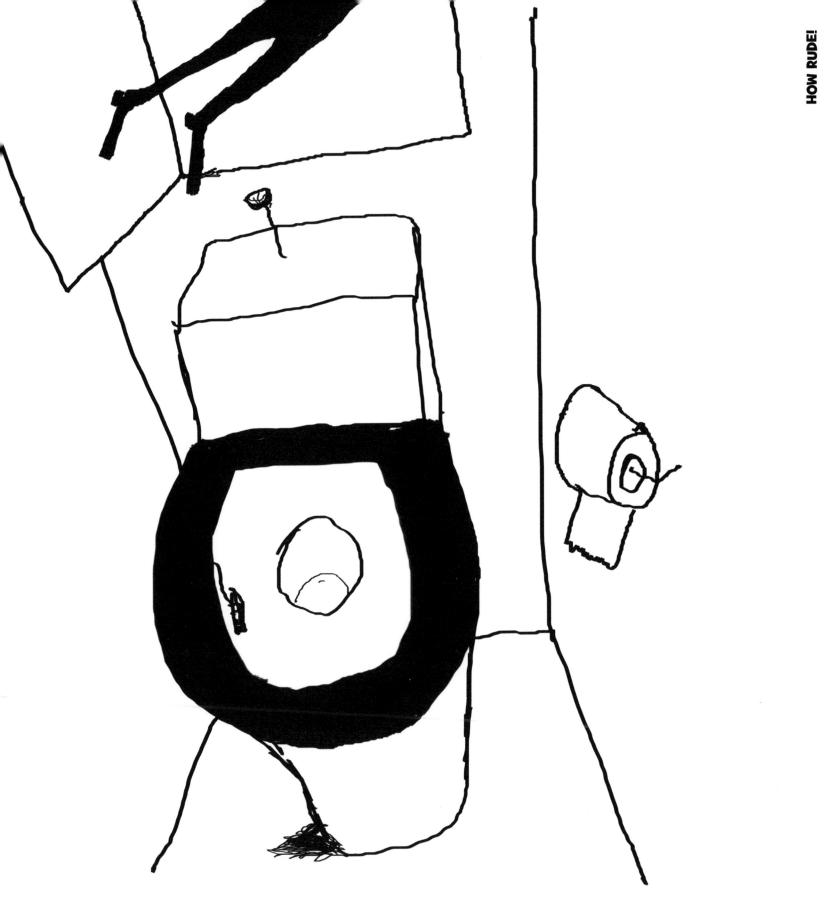

Super-Hurry left for a mission without flushing the toilet.
Flush it, then draw the water **swirling** down the toilet!

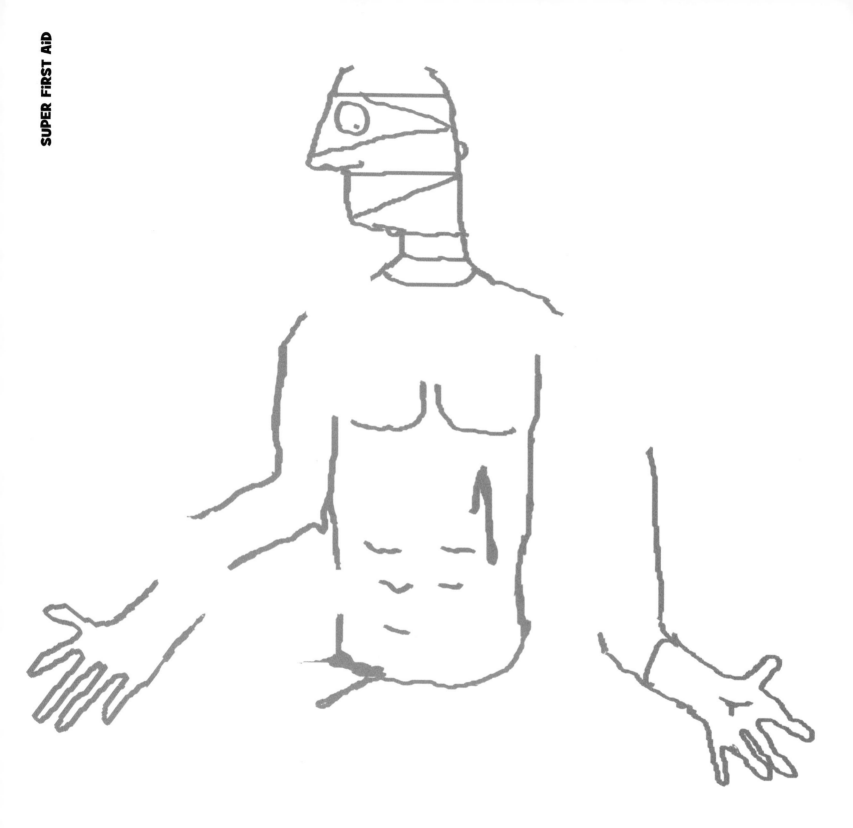

Treat Captain Clumsy's injuries by drawing him **bandages.**

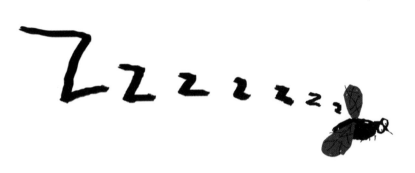

Draw a net around the nasty **Fly of Doom.**

(He may look small, but he's really evil!)

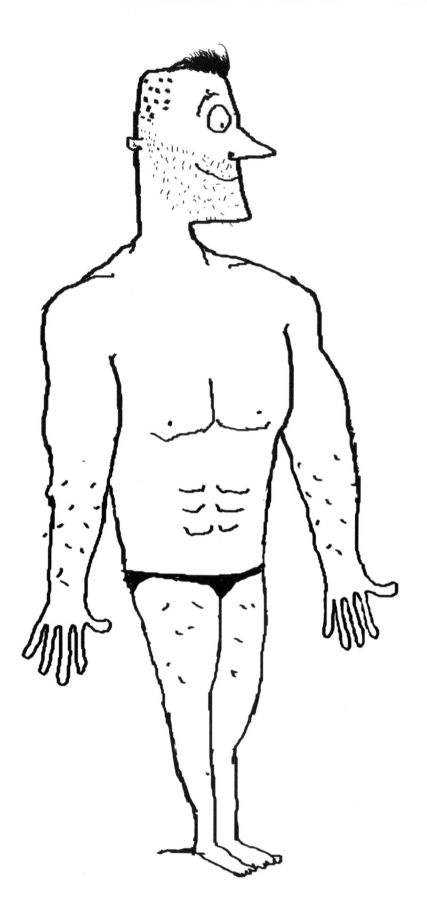

These heroes just woke up!

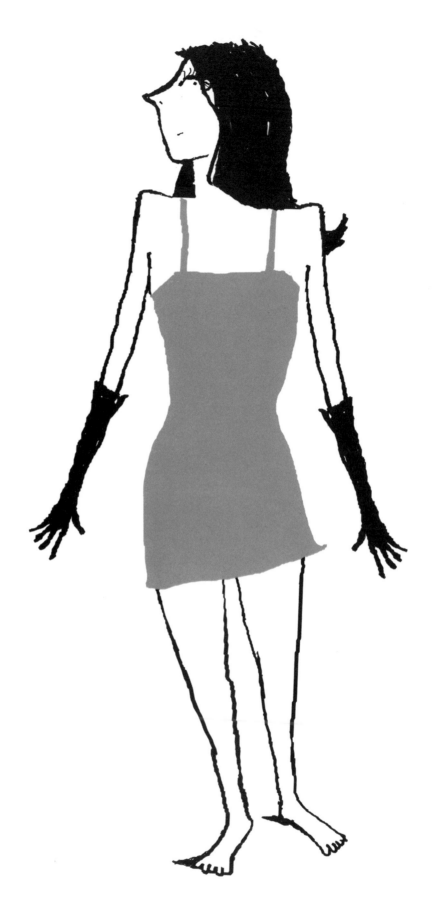

Get them dressed so they can go fight crime!

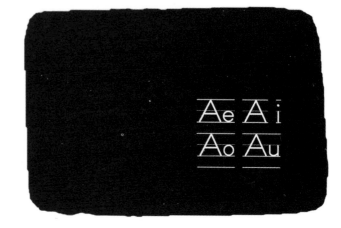

This superhero class is taught by the giant Teacher-Creature!
Draw it.

Draw Super-Suave, the **coolest** superhero around.

Color the Web Master's costume the **ugliest** colors you can find.

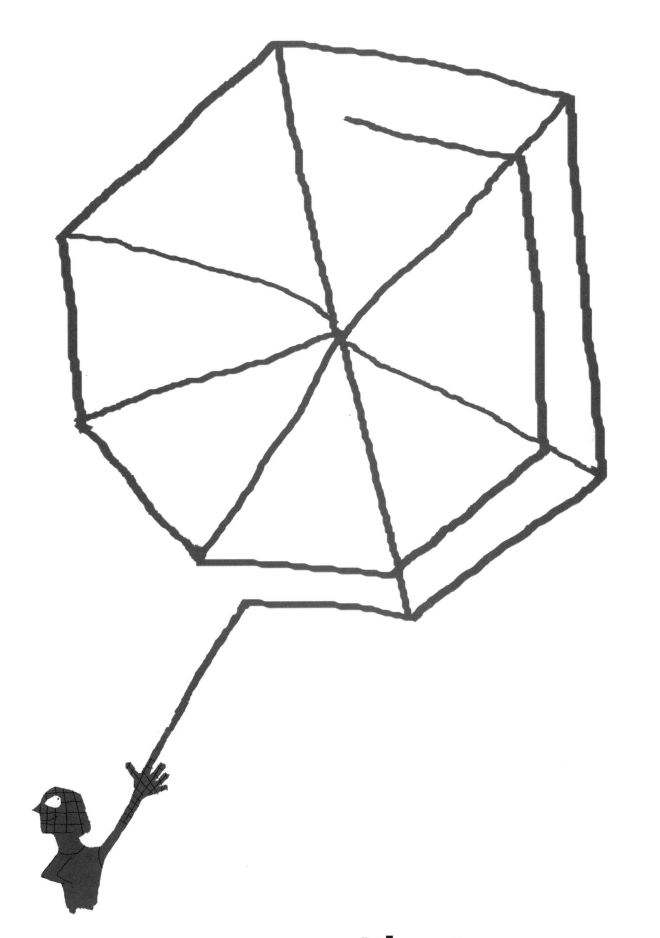

Finish drawing Arachno-Girl's web **without** lifting your pencil.

SUPER *shark*

Super Shark has lost his baby teeth. Draw him new teeth.

OCCUPIED!

HEROES
SAVE
THE WORLD

Cut out this sign and attach it to the **bathroom** door

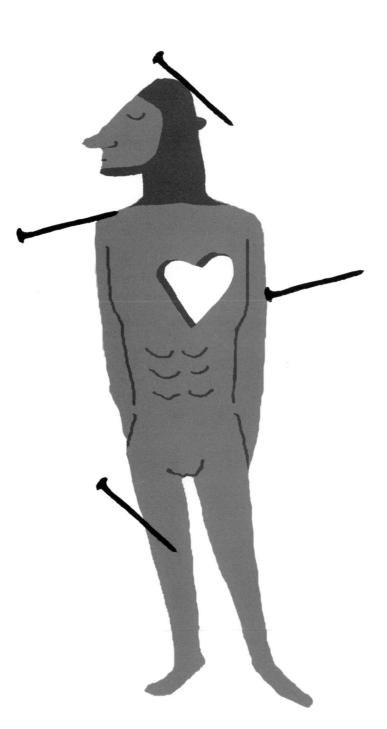

Super-Magnetic attracts metal.
Finish drawing nails all over his body.

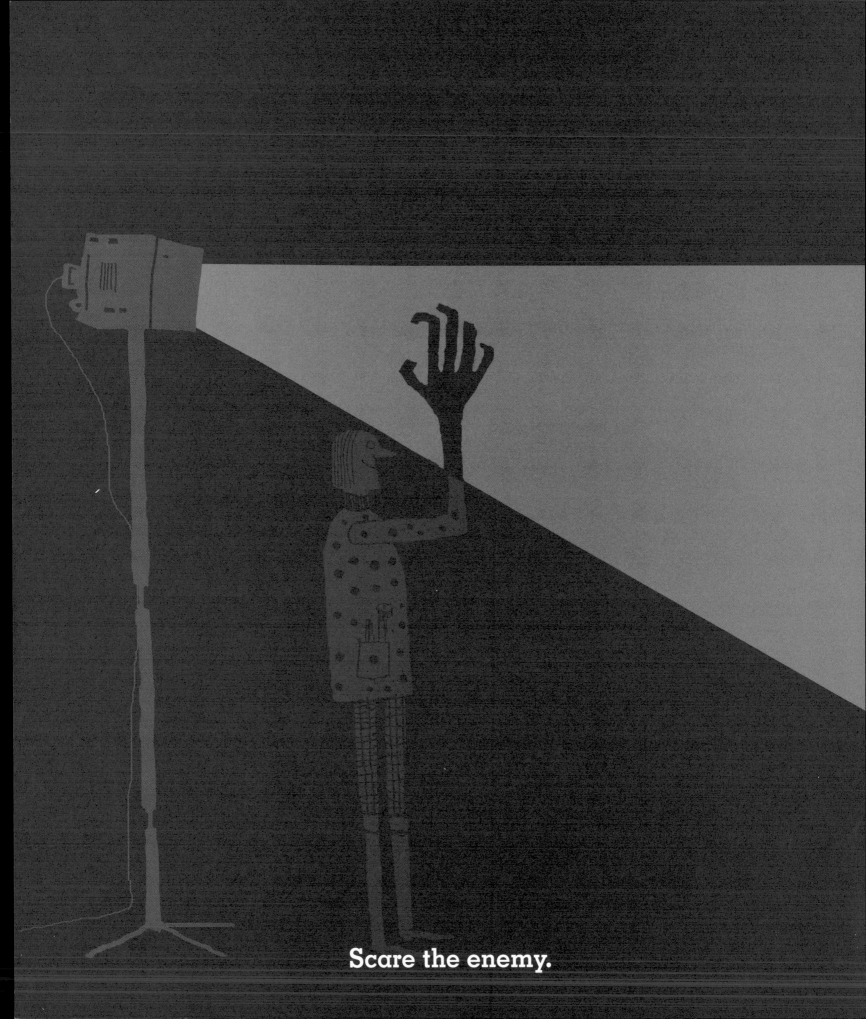

Scare the enemy.

Copy out the hand's **shadow** in the big spotlight.

Super-Urgent doesn't have the time to go to the bathroom.
Draw a puddle on the ground.

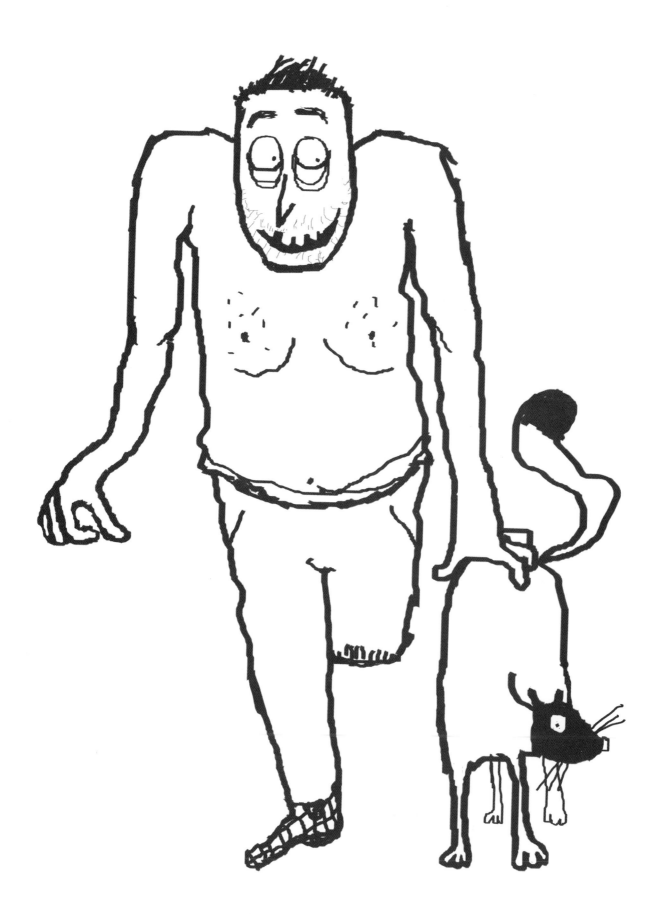

Draw scars and **tattoos** on this retired superhero.

Decorate Super-Woman's **crown.**

Cut out the page then fold it along the dotted lines.
Have fun squishing and stretching **Elasto-Boy.**

Yuck!

Draw bird poop all over this superhero.

Night falls over Darktown...

the villains can't be seen! Color the bad guys in black.

Draw **Double-Faced's** other face.

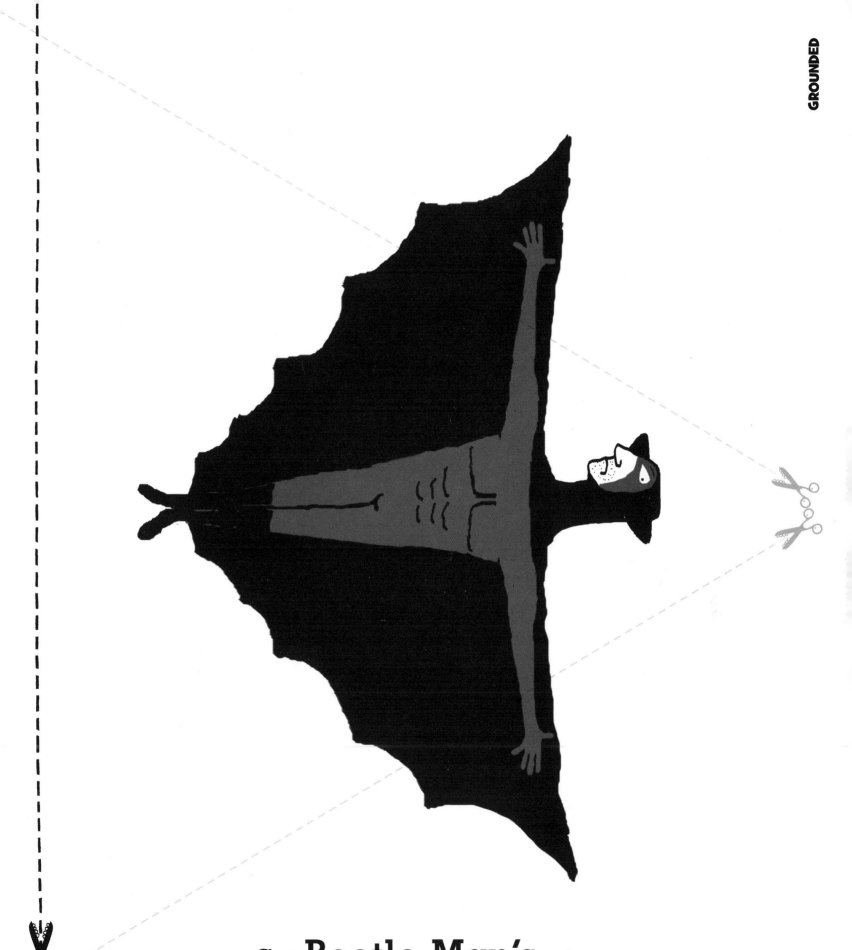

Cut **Beetle-Man's** wings.

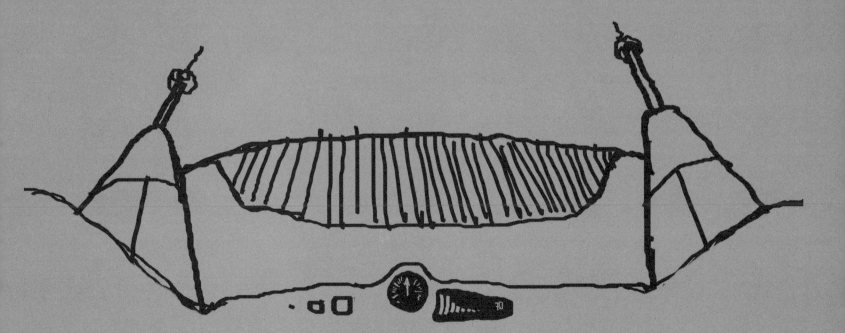

Draw laser beams to **damage** the villains' car.

The **Furry-Footed Fury** was just here.
Draw all of the footprints his furry feet left behind.

**The Lunk and the Human Stone are in a boat.
They're both seasick. Color them green.**

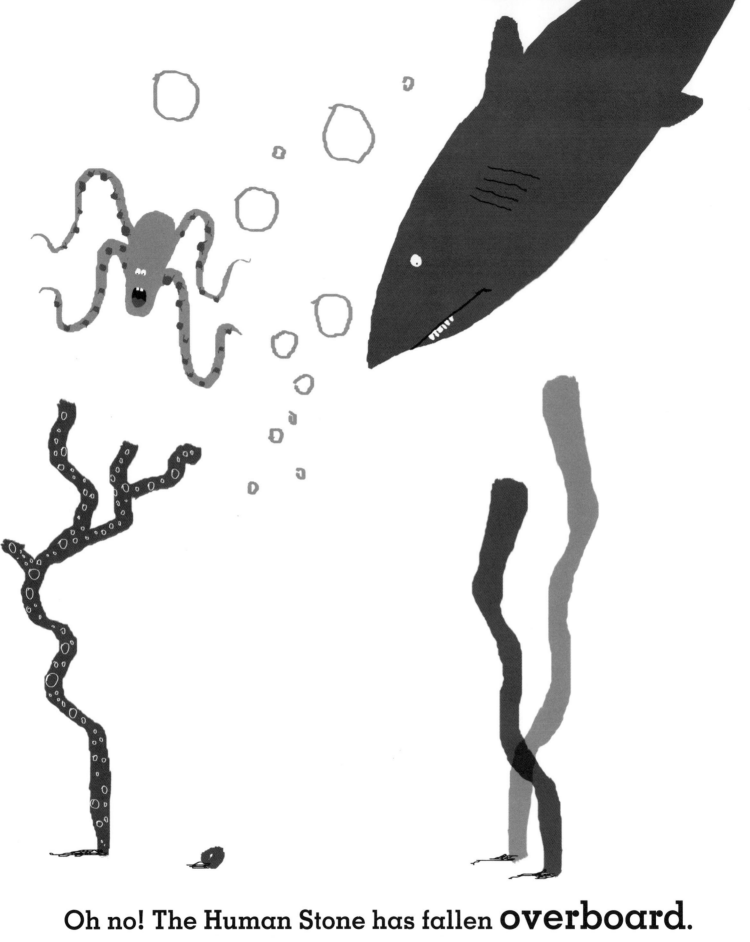

Oh no! The Human Stone has fallen **overboard.**
Draw him underwater.

Beetle-Man has lost his **wings**.
Connect the dots to see how he can fly.

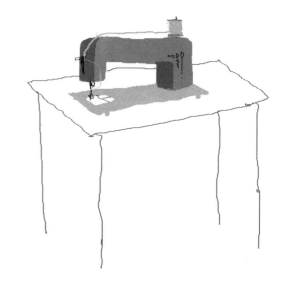

Your mom is making you a superhero costume,
but it's very ugly! Draw it.

THE CAPED
PERSUADER
YOU LOVE

Cut out this **postcard**, glue your picture on it,
then send it to your parents.

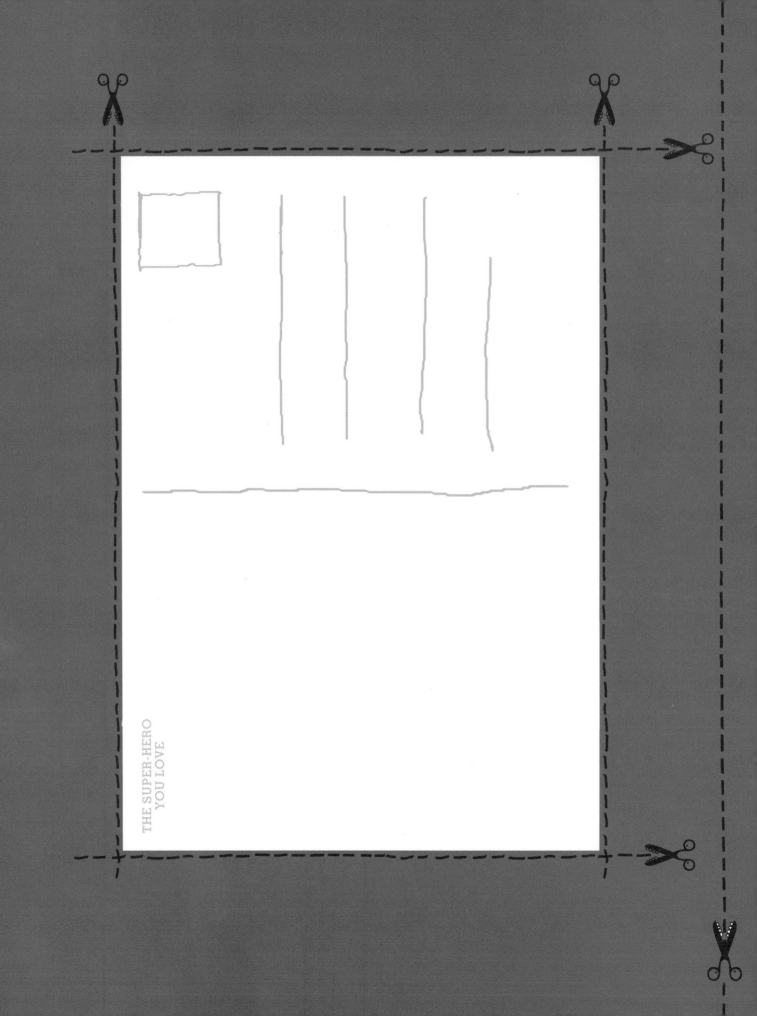

THE SUPER-HERO
YOU LOVE

Draw an awesome **button** for superheroes to wear.
Cut it out and tape it to your shirt.

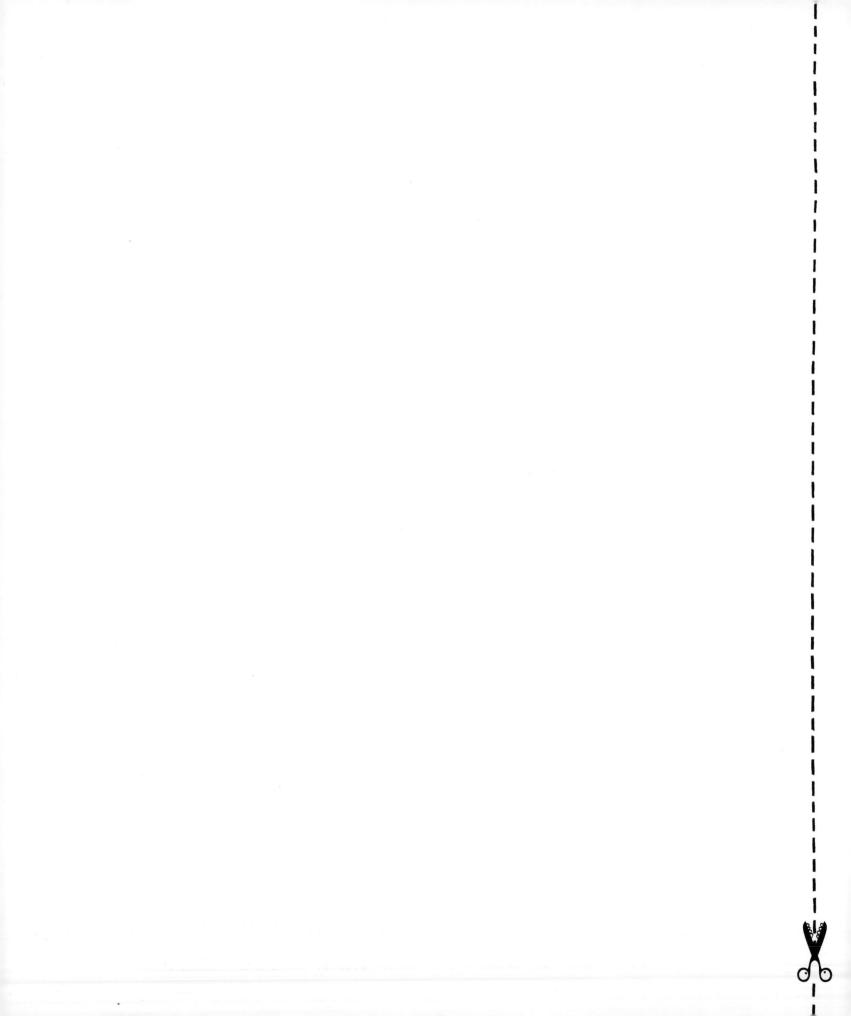

What do you think **Flying Man** forgot to wear this morning?
First, help him out by finishing his costume.

Now find Flying Man's **underwear** and circle them.

Color in the rest of his room.

Help the people cross the **city**

by avoiding the bad guys.

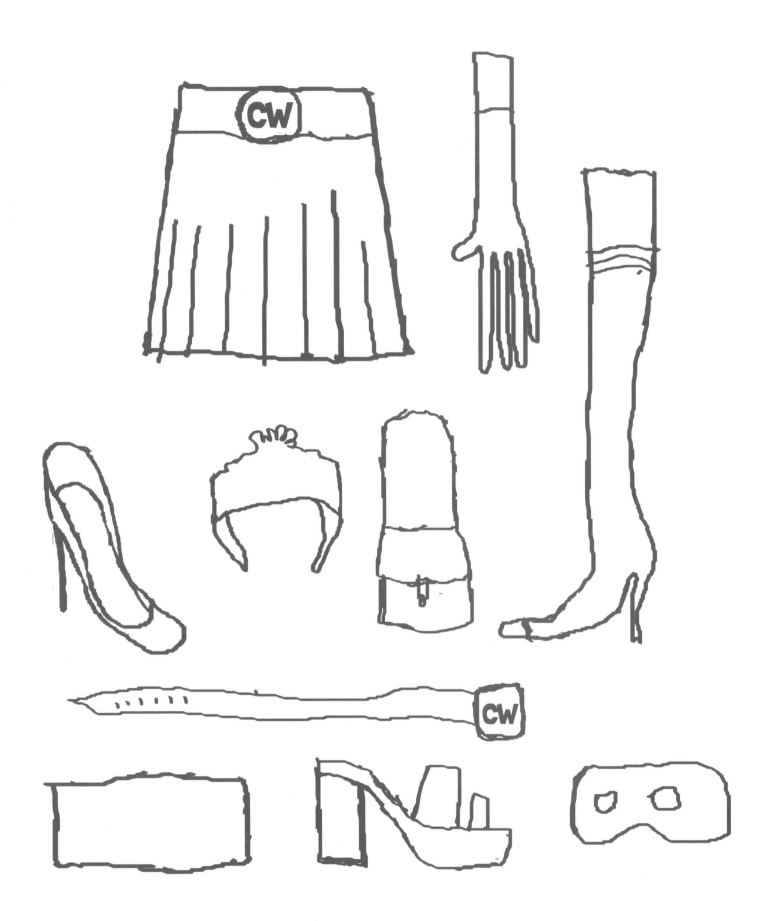

Catwalk-Woman loves fashion.

Color in her **wardrobe**.

Match each doll to the **hero** it belongs to.

It's the final **showdown!** Draw whatever you want.

Now draw who **won!**